F·E·A·R
ADVENTURE

THE EMERALD
PIRATE

JAK SHADOW

Wizard Books

Published in the UK in 2005
by Wizard Books, an imprint of Icon Books Ltd.,
The Old Dairy, Brook Road, Thriplow,
Cambridge SG8 7RG
email: wizard@iconbooks.co.uk
www.iconbooks.co.uk/wizard

Sold in the UK, Europe, South Africa
and Asia by Faber and Faber Ltd.,
3 Queen Square, London WC1N 3AU
or their agents

Distributed in the UK, Europe, South Africa
and Asia by TBS Ltd., Frating Distribution Centre,
Colchester Road, Frating Green, Colchester CO7 7DW

Published in Australia in 2005
by Allen & Unwin Pty. Ltd.,
PO Box 8500, 83 Alexander Street,
Crows Nest, NSW 2065

Distributed in Canada by
Penguin Books Canada,
90 Eglinton Avenue East, Suite 700,
Toronto, Ontario M4P 2Y3

ISBN 1 84046 690 1

Typesetting by Hands Fotoset

Printed and bound in the UK by
Clays of Bungay

Contents

Background

Last summer you went to a holiday adventure camp. It was fantastic! Instead of teachers, real soldiers, explorers and athletes taught you how to do all kinds of things. You learned how to survive in dangerous lands, how to abseil down a mountain and how to crack secret codes. They even taught you how to track someone cross-country and how to avoid being followed.

On your last day at the adventure camp you were awarded five certificates and told that you were one of the best students they had ever had. You remember that final evening as if it were yesterday and now, with your dangerous mission about to begin, you replay every detail of the scene in your head.

★ ★ ★

After a last campfire and a meal in the open air, one of the sergeants whispers in your ear.

'Colonel Strong would like to see you in his

office. Please follow me. There is nothing to worry about; you haven't done anything wrong.'

You saw Colonel Strong on your first day. He is the officer in charge of the camp, a big man with a booming voice who is more than a little terrifying.

You cannot stop your knees from trembling, and your hands feel cold and clammy as you walk towards his office. You are wondering what on Earth he wants to talk about.

'My people have been watching you all week,' Colonel Strong begins. 'I know you have had a great time here and you've done extremely well. We are all very proud of what you have been able to achieve.'

'It seems that you are exactly what we are looking for. Sit yourself down and let me explain,' he says, pointing to the chair.

'The world is in great danger. More danger than you could possibly imagine,' the colonel continues.

Why is the colonel talking to you like this? He obviously has more to say so you wait for him to continue.

'My organisation is fighting a secret war against an evil alien genius.'

'But who is he and what does he want?' you ask

'His name is Triton and he wants to rule the world,' the colonel tells you.

Colonel Strong passes you a photograph of Triton. He is like nothing you have ever seen before. He has green skin, piercing red eyes, pointed ears, a large nose and has strange

lumps on his face. You would have no trouble in picking him out in a crowd.

'I have checked out your history and I have watched you all week. I know that you are loyal, honest and brave, but even so I cannot tell you any more unless you swear a solemn oath to keep this secret.'

You are not too sure what the colonel means, but you know he is trustworthy and you long to hear more. You swear the solemn and binding oath that you will keep the secret.

'I work for an organisation called F.E.A.R.,' the colonel continues. 'It is an organisation so secret that only a handful of people in the whole world know about it.'

'But what is F.E.A.R.?' you ask.

'F.E.A.R. stands for Fighting Evil, Always Ready,' the colonel explains. 'I don't want you to feel you've been tricked but this activity camp was specially set up to recruit the ideal agent,' he continues. 'We selected only children who we knew would be brave, strong, honest and, above all, quick-witted. We have watched you this week, and out of all the children, you are the one we have picked. We want you to become a F.E.A.R. agent.'

'Agent! What sort of agent? A secret agent?' you shout.

'Yes, a very secret agent. But I can only tell you more if you agree to join us. Or would you prefer it if we just forgot this conversation?'

'Of course I want to help, but I'm only a child. What could I possibly do?' you ask.

'All of our agents are children now. Triton has captured all our best adult agents but he does not yet suspect our children.'

'Why can't we just hunt him down and kill him?' you reply.

'I wish it were that easy. The world Triton comes from is millions of miles from our planet, but somehow he has managed to get to Earth. He has a time machine and he is trying to change our time and our future. We have to stop him. We managed to capture one of his time machines and we've copied it so now we've got one of our own.'

'You can count on me,' you say, smiling at the colonel.

'If you agree to become a F.E.A.R. agent you will begin your training during the school holidays. You have been sworn to secrecy, and must not tell anyone about the work you are doing. We will tell your parents as much as they need to know, but no more.'

★ ★ ★

Over the holidays since, your training has been completed. You have worked hard and learned much. You know more about Triton now, especially the fact that he uses a time chip to take him back to a particular time and place. If you can take it from him, or destroy it, he will have to leave. F.E.A.R. have made a chip locator and on every mission you will take one with you. It will help you to find Triton.

Now you are ready to begin your mission, but Colonel Strong's words are ringing in your ears: 'Remember you are facing a most dangerous challenge and an evil enemy'.

You wait for your instructions.

How to Play

Before you start, the colonel will tell you as much as F.E.A.R. knows about Triton's plans.

This is not like a normal book. Each section of the book is numbered. At the end of each section you will have a choice to make. Each of these choices will send you to a different section of the book. You make the choices and decide how you are going to deal with Triton.

If you fail, your mission will end and Triton will be able to continue his plan to take over the world. If you manage to combat all of the dangers Triton presents you will defeat him and the world will be safe – until he strikes in another time and another place! The world needs you.

Your Mission

When you arrive at the F.E.A.R. base Colonel Strong meets you. He seems to be a worried man. He doesn't say very much until you are safely in the mission room.

'I've got lots to tell you and we don't have much time. This could be an even more difficult mission than you or I were expecting. We are going to send you back 300 years, but first we've got to fly to a little island called Santa Diana, off the coast of Cuba.'

'What? Where? How?' you stumble, full of questions.

'We have a time machine on a ship in the harbour there. Come on, let's go. I'll explain everything on the way,' the colonel urges.

Colonel Strong fills your head with as much information as he can tell you. Two days ago one of his agents was sent back in time to the island. All Strong knows is that the agent has gone missing. They know he is safe, but they just can't get to him at the moment. The last report was that Triton has become a pirate captain. His pirates are attacking ships and are about to destroy Santa Diana's pretty, peaceful port.

'Why is he interested in Santa Diana?' you ask.

'In our time Santa Diana is the most important navy base in the world. If Triton can capture Santa Diana in the past, he can send his men forward into the future to capture and destroy the base. It will leave the world at his mercy. He must be stopped!' Colonel Strong explains.

When you reach Santa Diana you see how important the little island has become. The harbour is full of warships, preparing themselves for an attack by Triton's pirates if he manages to succeed in carrying out his plan.

10

Colonel Strong takes you to a huge warship.
All of the crew are F.E.A.R. agents. Deep
inside the ship is a strange chamber,
surrounded by computers, screens and
switches.

'This is our most closely guarded secret.'
Colonel Strong tells you. 'It is our time
machine. It is a copy of a machine that we
captured from Triton when he was in ancient
Egypt. We know it works and we are going to
use this to send you back to Santa Diana in the
year 1720.'

Colonel Strong gives you a strange looking
object, which looks a little like a mobile phone.

'This is your chip locator. It will help you
find Triton's time chip,' he explains. 'You can
also take one other thing with you. I will leave
you to decide which item

will be of most
use to you. I have
left all the items
on the table.'

You walk over to the table and see a compass, a telescope and a bag of gold coins.

'Before you make your decision, we had better dress you up like a cabin boy,' says the colonel. 'Jeans and a t-shirt and those trainers will make you stick out like a sore thumb in 1720!'

Now read paragraph **1** to begin your adventure.

The Emerald Pirate

1

You disappear behind a screen and find your
clothes laid out ready for you. There is a rough
pair of ragged trousers and a dirty, white shirt.
On the floor is a pair of old-fashioned shoes
with a metal buckle. There is also a broad belt
with a small pouch on it.

You quickly change into your costume and
walk over to the table, where Colonel Strong is
looking through the telescope.

The compass will help you know which way
you are heading. The telescope might be useful
if you need to see what is in the distance. The
bag of coins might be handy if you need to buy
something. It is up to you. What do you think
would be of most use to you?

If you choose the compass, go to **91**. If you
prefer the telescope, go to **5**. If you think the
bag of coins would be more useful, go to **12**.

2

You can see flashes of light through the trees in front of you. It is Triton. Just as you turn the corner you hear a strange, humming noise and then there is another flash of light. You get there just in time to see Triton's time machine flicker then disappear into the future. You have failed. He has escaped, but he has not destroyed Santa Diana.

Suddenly you feel yourself falling, falling, falling.

You find yourself on the floor of the time chamber and see Colonel Strong's face peering through the glass. Your mission is over. Strong promised that you would not come to any harm and he has kept his promise. The colonel opens the door and helps you to your feet.

'I was so close to catching Triton' you tell him. 'I think I know how to complete the mission.'

If you would like to try again, go back to **1**.

3

'We do have another surprise for Green. The zombie king is hunting his fleet and I'm sure that they will help us,' you say to Mary Grey and the mayor.

'Excellent!' says the mayor.

'Let's find him out and wreck his ships,' says Mary Grey. Now go to **97**.

4

The *Roaring Girl* turns to chase the *Emerald Dragon*. You can see Green pacing the deck, shouting at his men. But you are gaining on him. The *Emerald Dragon* suddenly stops and many of Green's crew jump over the side. 'He's hit the rocks!' you shout.

The crew of the *Roaring Girl* cheer, but
as you watch the *Emerald Dragon* begin to
sink you can see Green climbing into a lifeboat.
He must not escape.

Should the *Roaring Girl* fire her cannons at
him? If so, go to **90**. If you think you should
get into a rowing boat and follow him,
go to **47**.

5

The pocket telescope works just like binoculars
and will help you see into the distance. If you
are at sea you will be able to spot other ships or
islands and if you are at the top of a hill you
should be able to
see for miles. This will
be very useful to help you avoid dangers
and you should be able to see others before
they see you.

'I think I'll take the telescope,' you say.

'That could be very useful,' says the colonel,
smiling.

The telescope fits into your pouch, alongside the chip locator. Now turn to **16**.

6

Peering through a hole in the wardrobe door, you can see that the captain's cabin is now full of the most evil-looking collection of pirates that you could imagine. They are the captains of his fleet of pirate ships. Green has spread out

a chart of the nearby islands and is pointing at it as he explains his plan to them.

'First we stop and sink any ships in the area. Then we move towards Santa Diana. I want the whole island to become our new base. I am not interested in the gold they have hidden there. All I ask is that you destroy the town.'

So, Triton plans to attack Santa Diana. But this has still not helped you find his time chip. Until you do you cannot stop him. Now go to **18**.

7

The *Roaring Girl* makes fast progress to Santa Diana. The townsfolk hide as the pirate ship pulls alongside the jetty. Mary Grey sends some of her men to the town to tell the people that they have nothing to fear. They are terrified but soon realise that Mary Grey's pirates are here to help them.

The mayor and several of the townsfolk arrive at the jetty and you join them with Mary Grey to make your plans.

Will you suggest that the *Roaring Girl* and her crew attack Green when he arrives? If so, go to **87**. If you think it would be a better idea to hide the *Roaring Girl* and take the cannons off the ship and carry them up to the top of the hill, turn to **20**.

8

You manage to catch just enough water to fill your water bottle. By only allowing yourself a sip each hour you manage to survive. The storm has driven you quite a distance, but you still cannot see land. Do you have a telescope? If you do have a telescope then turn to **76**. If you do not have a telescope then turn to **92**.

9

You take out your compass and quickly look at the chart beside the wheel.

'Where are we?'
you shout.

'About here,'
says Rupert

pointing to the chart, 'but I'm not quite sure.'

'I think we're heading for some reefs,' you say.

'You're right. We had better steer around them,' says Rupert.

While Rupert tries to look at the chart, you check your compass. You see that if you don't turn soon you will hit the reef and possibly sink. You take the wheel and turn the ship quickly. You have just missed the reefs by the skin of your teeth and the *Dragonfly* heads off towards a nearby island. Now go to **31**.

10

'I think we'd better head for Santa Diana. Green may still attack the island,' you say and Mary Grey agrees with you.

The *Roaring Girl* turns around and makes for Santa Diana. Now go to 7.

11

Your decision to make for Santa Diana is a brave one, as you have little food and water. The sun is beating down on you and making you feel sleepy. But you dare not sleep. The sail is barely moving as there is so little wind and the lifeboat is only travelling very slowly.

You sip the last few drops of your water and realise that if you do not find land soon then you will be doomed.

Suddenly the waves begin to whip up and there is a wind. Great forks of lightning strike above you and it begins to rain. You tip your head backwards and open your mouth, grateful for the few drops of rain that trickle down your throat. Perhaps there is a chance! If you were to take down the sail and hold it out in front of you, you could catch some rain. But this would mean that you would not make any progress. If you wish to take down the sail, turn to **8**. If you wish to use the strong wind to help you get to Santa Diana more quickly, turn to **92**.

12

You open the bag and pour the coins into your hand. They are large, gold coins with the face of George I on one side. There are ten of them. These should come in handy. Pirates are always greedy for gold.

'I think the coins will be the most useful,' you tell the colonel.

'Yes, they could be. Ten of those coins will buy you a great deal in the past,' the colonel agrees.

You manage to fit the bag of coins into your pouch, along with the chip locator. Now turn to **16**.

13

You decide against offering to make a drink for the captain and instead you set about tidying up his cabin. There is dust and muck everywhere. After a short while the captain, who has been studying charts on his desk, groans and stands up.

'I'm going ashore, young one. I need to speak with my captains. We've got much to plan.'

With that he leaves the cabin and you can hear him stomping up the stairs towards the deck. You can hear shouts in the distance and realise it is now your chance to look around his cabin and see if you can find his time chip. You switch on your chip locator. It is flashing and beeping furiously. Now go to **58**.

14

You decide to run for it. No sooner have you left the cabin than you run straight into one of Captain Green's crew. He grabs you and

although you struggle to break
his hold, you cannot
get free. Captain Green
appears.

'A spy,' says Green.
'You know what we do
with spies. Make him walk the plank!'

The pirate, followed by Green, takes you on
deck. Another pirate pushes out a plank over
the sea. The pirate shoves you onto the plank
and tells you to walk. There is no escape. You
begin to walk until you reach the end of the
plank and then take one last step. Strange
shapes pass before your eyes and you feel
yourself falling, falling, falling.

You find yourself on the floor of the time
chamber and see Colonel Strong's face peering
through the glass. Your mission is over.
Strong promised that you would not come to
any harm and he has kept his promise. The
colonel opens the door and helps you to
your feet.

'You've still got plenty of time to catch Triton,' he says.

If you would like to try the mission once again, go back to **1**.

15

The zombies are close behind you and you decide to risk crossing the bridge. As you take your first footstep onto it, it begins to sway and creek. The zombies are now at the end of the bridge, but won't cross it. Perhaps they know something that you do not? You take another step and the plank beneath your foot cracks and breaks. You feel yourself falling, falling, falling.

You find yourself on the floor of the time chamber and see Colonel Strong's face peering through the glass. Your mission is over. Strong promised that you would not come to any harm and he has kept his promise. The colonel opens the door and helps you to your feet.

'You were doing so well,' he says. 'You were getting close to the time chip and there's still time for you to catch Triton.'

If you would like to try the mission once again, go back to **1**.

16

'Is everything ready?' shouts the colonel.

All of the agents in the room nod their agreement, or give the 'thumbs up' sign to the colonel. The time machine has been powered up for you.

'I'm told it feels rather like falling. You might feel a little bit sick, but you can't come to any harm,' the colonel tells you. 'You'll need to swallow this tracker. It will tell us where you are and, most importantly, if you get into any serious difficulties we can bring you back straight away.'

You swallow a tiny capsule and wash it down with a sip of water that the colonel has handed you.

'There is just one thing, colonel' you say. 'We're on a boat, in the harbour and if I go back 300 years I'll end up in the water, won't I?'

'Hadn't thought of that,' says the colonel. 'How far will he be from the shore?' the colonel asks the nearest agent.

'Not far,' he replies. 'He can swim, can't he?'

You nod that you can swim. At least the water will be warm.

'One last thing,' says the colonel. 'I don't want you worrying about our other agent. We know where he is and he is not in any danger. Triton has left him on a desert island and after you've gone I'll send some men back to get him.'

You step inside the chamber and take a deep breath. Suddenly the chamber feels as if it is spinning. Your view through the glass begins to fade and swirling shapes float around you. You hear a strange, whooshing sound, as if a strong wind has blown up. The spinning continues for a few more seconds and then you feel yourself falling. Now turn to **24**.

17

You take out your compass and work out which way is north. Santa Diana lies to the east, but

from what you can remember from the chart, there is

another island closer, just to the south. You quickly check your food and water and realise that you probably do not have enough to reach Santa Diana. Do you want to make for Santa Diana? If so, go to **11**. If you think it would be better to try to find more food and water and head for the nearby island, go to **78**.

18

The meeting of the pirate captains is over. They all agree to follow his plans. Green follows them out of the cabin and you are alone, except of course for the parrot. You decide to feed him a few seeds, just to keep him quiet. If he squawks too much someone might come and investigate. As you begin handing him seeds you see that he has a chain around one of his feet and attached to the chain is a key. The parrot  is happy now that he has some food and you bend down and unclip the key from the chain and wonder which of the locks it fits. You do not have much time so you begin to search for the right lock. Now go to **73**.

19

The zombies take you into their camp. It is dirty and smelly and there are zombies everywhere. Ahead of you is a ruined house, surrounded by torches stuck into the ground. A zombie sits on a chair with a crown on his head. He must be the king of the zombies.

'Welcome. We wish you no harm. All of my people were sailors until Green and his pirates sunk their ships. We are all afraid. We want to help you. What do you know about Green?' he says slowly.

Leaving out the fact that Green is in fact an evil alien called Triton, you tell the zombie king that Green wants to destroy Santa Diana.

'We will help you,' he says when you have finished.

Now turn to **88**.

20

The crew of the *Roaring Girl* and the townsfolk drag the cannons up the steep slope and place them on top of the hill. From this position you can see the jetty. You manage to get the cannons ready only just in time as Green's fleet comes into view.

The first of his ships heads towards the jetty and you wait until they have got closer.

'Fire!' you shout and the cannons bark, sending huge metal balls towards Green's ships.

The first ships are hit and begin to sink, but the rest of Green's pirates are still heading for the island. Quickly the cannons are reloaded and they fire again, sinking more of Green's ships. But Green's own ship, the *Emerald Dragon*, has turned and is heading out to sea. You must chase him.

Mary Grey calls her crew together and you race down the hill, towards the *Roaring Girl*, which is anchored in the bay near the jetty. In minutes you are underway and chasing the *Emerald Dragon*. Now turn to **4**.

21

'Another chest?' Triton bellows. 'Where?'

'Over there,' you shout. 'Look!' It is nothing but a pile of coconuts, but in the dense jungle it does look like a chest. He is greedy for the gold and begins to run towards it.

You seize your chance and run towards his time machine. There is a bright, flashing panel near a set of switches and buttons. In the middle is his time chip. Will you grab the time chip and fit it into your chip locator? If so, go to **61**. Or will you throw the time chip into the jungle? If so, go to **41**.

22

You manage to grab a few minutes' sleep in your cabin, but are woken by men running on the deck above you. There is much shouting and cheering. You hear a knock on your door and when you open it one of the pirate crew is standing there.

'The captain wants you on deck. You and all of the new crewmen. You've got to sign the articles of war and swear your life to the captain.'

 Triton must have
recruited some other
crewmen quite
recently, so at least
you'll not be alone in
facing the captain. You quickly make sure that
your chip locator is turned off and follow the
crewman up the stairs and onto the deck.
You join the rest of the new crew members in a
line and Captain Green paces up and down in
front of you.

'You're all new crew and welcome. But
before we sail you must swear the articles of
war to me and pledge your lives to your captain
and to your ship.'

One by one the new crewmen swear their
lives to the captain and he paints a red cross on
their chests.

As he stands in front of you it is now your
turn and you realise that it is not red paint, but
blood. Will you agree to swear your life to
Triton? If so, go to **62**. If you refuse, turn to **69**.

23

As the guard approaches you hide in the lifeboat, pulling a canvas cover over you. He passes without giving you or the lifeboat a second look. You wait a few seconds, hearing his footsteps disappear into the distance.

Pulling the canvas aside, you climb back out of the lifeboat and continue lowering it into the water. You have only a few minutes before he will reach your side of the ship again. So you quickly untie the lifeboat from the ropes and push it away from the *Emerald Dragon*. You carefully paddle the lifeboat away and in a few minutes you have drifted out of sight and into the darkness.

You continue drifting for several hours. The sunrise brings some daylight, but you have no idea where you are. Do you have a compass? If you do have a compass, turn to **17**. If you do not have a compass, turn to **94**.

24

You hardly dare to look down. But as you do look down you see sparkling, clear water below you. Your fall takes you under, but the water is not very deep and as soon as your feet hit the bottom you spring straight back up to the surface. You look around.

Colonel Strong, the time chamber, the huge ship and all the warships have gone. The harbour has disappeared and all you can see is a beautiful beach, with the waves gently lapping onto the white sand. Just ahead of you is a long, wooden platform, called a jetty, which is held up by trunks of wood sunk into the seabed. There is a small sailing boat and a man, sitting half-asleep, with a fishing rod in his hand.

You check to see that your pouch is still closed. Everything is safe and you slowly swim towards the jetty, heading for a wooden ladder. The man has still not spotted you and you climb up the ladder, soaking wet.

Do you want to wake up the fisherman? If so, go to **81**. If you want to ignore him and walk into the town, go to **27**.

25

'Where's the *Emerald Dragon*? Have we changed course?' bellows Captain George.

'Yes, Captain,' replies the first mate.

While the captain and the crewmen argue, you look at your compass and realise that you are headed for a small desert island, if you have understood the chart beside the wheel. You have lost the *Emerald Dragon* and you have no idea which direction Captain Green was headed. Now turn to **31**.

26

You crawl underneath a thorny bush, pull some coconut palm leaves over you and wait to see what happens. After a few minutes you can see the light of several torches coming in your direction and the drumming is getting louder.

Now you can hear a strange moaning noise, but you still can see nothing apart from the torchlight. A few more minutes pass. The drumming and the moaning are getting louder.

Along the path you can now see a figure holding a torch. It is a horrible sight. It has blank eyes and is moaning. You never thought that this could be possible, but it is one of the living dead.

More figures come into view, dozens of them, and all holding torches. Some have drums and all of them are moaning this terrible sound. You are terrified. What will you do? If you wish to continue to hide, turn to **74**. If you think it is best to run, turn to **38**.

27

It is a short and pleasant walk towards the town. The island is covered with coconut trees and you can hear parrots squawking. It is a beautiful, hot sunny day and you are enjoying your stroll, which beats a rainy school holiday back home.

As you walk along the path you can see a wooden wall ahead with a sleepy soldier standing guard. He doesn't even wake up as you pass through the gate and into the town. There are not very many people around and the houses are small and empty. You can hear voices in the distance and you head towards these sounds.

You enter a square and it seems that everyone who lives in Santa Diana is there. The leader, who introduces himself as Mayor Mason, is asking for helpers to set out in a ship to try to find Captain Green and his pirates. The mayor's son, Rupert, will be the captain on this ship. The pirates are about to attack the island and the mayor has collected as much gold as he can find to give to the pirates to tempt them into leaving Santa Diana alone.

With what you know about his plans, you figure out that Captain Green must be Triton. Will you offer to help on this mission? If so, go to **70**. If you decide this is not the best plan and want to have a better look around the island first, go to **75**.

28

As you peer over the edge you can see several sharks circling below. The pirate pushes you forward with his sword until you reach the end of the plank. You decide to jump rather than be pushed and suddenly you feel yourself falling, falling, falling.

You find yourself on the floor of the time chamber and see Colonel Strong's face peering through the glass. Your mission is over. Strong promised that you would not come to any harm and he has kept his promise. The colonel opens the door and helps you to your feet.

'You were doing so well,' he says. 'You were getting close to the time chip and there's still time for you to catch Triton.'

If you would like to try the mission once again, go back to **1**.

29

With the *Roaring Girl* safely hidden, you and Mary Grey help the townsfolk prepare for

Green's attack. Suddenly there is a shout from one of the lookouts. He has seen several ships heading towards the island. Is it Green? You grab a telescope and peer through it, trying to make out whether it is the *Emerald Dragon*.

'I don't recognise them. Who are they?' you ask.

Mary Grey looks through the telescope. 'It's the zombie king! Now we're in trouble!' she shouts.

One of the ships comes in alongside the jetty and a strange figure steps ashore. He is a huge man with a blank expression on his face. He wears a crown on his head.

'I wish you no harm,' he says slowly. 'We are all sailors. Green sank our ships. And now we will sink his. We will help you all we can.'

Everyone makes final preparations. Green's fleet has been sighted near Santa Diana. The zombie king takes his fleet to find Green, and you and Mary climb a steep hill to try to see what is happening.

Holding a telescope to your eye, you look in every direction to see if you can find Green's fleet. In the far distance you see smoke and hear cannons being fired. It is a sea battle. The zombie king has attacked Green's pirates. Some of the pirate ships have toppled over and begin to sink. You look to see if you can find Green's own ship, the *Emerald Dragon*.

It has slipped away from the battle. Will you hop aboard the *Roaring Girl* and chase it? If so, go to **4**. But the ship might be headed towards Santa Diana. Should you take the cannons off the *Roaring Girl* and try to use them against Green? If you think this is a better idea, go to **20**.

30

You head off down the right trail. He has obviously gone this way. You can see his strange barefoot prints in the earth. Where is he heading? And how far ahead is he? Do you want to run and try to catch him up? If so, go to **72**. Or do you think it is better to go more slowly in case he is waiting to attack you? If so, go to **2**.

31

The ship anchors just offshore and you and your crewmates swim to the land.

'We need fresh food and water,' one says. 'Why don't you go inland and see if there is anyone on the island?'

You nod in agreement and head across the beach, finding a trail leading uphill. At least from here you should be able to see whether anyone else is on the island.

After a few minutes of hard climbing you reach the top of the hill and look back towards the beach. To your horror you see that the ship has left. At least the crew have left you a lifeboat so that you can make your own way to wherever you want to go. Now go to **82**.

32

Once the *Dragonfly* has passed the dangerous rocks and reef near the island, it turns and heads around the island, making for the first place to hunt for Triton. No sooner has the ship made the turn, than you see, heading towards you, a large boat with brightly dressed men onboard. They are shouting at you, but you cannot hear them properly because of the sound of the waves.

'We'd better surrender,' says Rupert, and the other men onboard agree with him.

'Who are they?' you ask. 'Is it Captain Green?'

'No, lad. They are Maroons, escaped slaves, but they're pirates all the same,' replies Rupert.

The Maroon ship pulls alongside you. Now go to **36**.

33

With a sweep of his sword, Captain George knocks your sword out of your hand. He stands back and smiles.

'I won't harm you. But you'll have to leave the ship,' he tells you.

The Maroons load food and water onto a lifeboat and lower you down into it.

'Good luck,' says Captain George as he pushes your lifeboat away from the *Red Lady*.

The wind and waves take you away from the *Red Lady* and your lifeboat drifts into the distance. The *Red Lady* has disappeared from view, but after an hour or so you see a speck in the distance. Is it another ship? After a while you realise it is an island. Now go to **78**.

34

The zombie king sends some of his men to collect food and water for you. You walk with him back to the beach and find your lifeboat. Although he is rather smelly and odd, you realise you like the zombie king and are happy to shake his hand as he wishes you good luck. He even gives you a telescope as a gift.

The zombies push your boat into the water and a strong wind takes you out to sea. Once you have cleared the island the wind dies down and your boat begins to drift. You are very, very thirsty, even after drinking all the water. Suddenly a storm whips up and tosses the boat this way and that. With your water gone and your food washed over the side by the waves, you know you cannot last very long. You can either hope that the storm passes and you can survive. If so, go to **92**. Or you can try to catch some water by using the sail. If so, go to **8**.

35

'Set sail for Santa Diana!' you shout.

'Aye, aye Captain,' shouts the first mate.

The *Red Lady* begins to make good progress towards Santa Diana, but the crew are talking behind your back. Although you are now the captain, they are more frightened of Green than you.

A group of them are busily talking and the first mate walks across to you and says, 'Captain, the crew won't go to Santa Diana. And they won't fight Green. I'm sorry sir. You'll have to take your chances in a lifeboat.'

The first mate gives you a compass, some food and water and they cast you adrift in a tiny lifeboat. In minutes the *Red Lady* has

disappeared into the distance, but you don't
have any real idea where you are. Now
turn to **17**.

36

The captain of the Maroons jumps aboard the
Dragonfly. He is a huge man, with enormous
earrings. There is a red scarf with white dots
tied around his head and he is wearing purple
trousers and a gold waistcoat. He has a curved
sword in his hand and a pistol stuck in his belt.

'Gentlemen,' he says, 'my name is Captain
George, master of the *Red Lady* and you are

my prisoners. Drop your weapons and you'll come to no harm.'

Several of the *Dragonfly's* crew drop their pistols, not that they were going to put up a fight anyway. A Maroon walks up to you and seems interested to find out whether you have any money in your pouch.

If you have a bag of coins, go to **63**. If you do not have a bag of coins, go to **42**.

37

'My name's Hop-Along Jones, pleased to meet you. Do you like my boat, the *Dashing Darling*?' the one-legged man asks you.

'Yes it's lovely. What are you doing here?' you ask.

'Well that would be telling wouldn't it? Do you want a real adventure young man? Have you ever thought of a life on the sea?'

'What do you mean?' you ask, frowning.

'I'm a pirate, lad. I'm one of Captain Green's finest men. Will you join me? We'll be back here

soon enough and when we do
there'll be plenty of gold
for all of us.'
Will you decide to join
Jones? Perhaps this
Captain Green is
Triton? If so, go to **51**. If
you decide against this, go to **57**.

38

Terrified, you wriggle out from under the bush
and run past the first zombie, crashing through
the jungle. It is difficult to run very fast. Vines
and creepers block your way and make you
trip and fall. The zombies are following
you. You can hear their moaning and when you
look behind you, you can see their torchlight.

You continue running for what feels like
hours, but still the zombies follow. Suddenly the
jungle stops and you find yourself facing a
wooden bridge. It is over a deep canyon in the
island. You can hear rushing water below.

Will you run across the bridge? If so, go to **15**. Or will you stop and let the zombies capture you? If so, go to **48**.

39

You climb up the rigging. Captain George follows you with his sword held between his teeth. The crew is shouting and cheering. You make it to the top of the sail, with the captain just behind you. Carefully holding onto the ropes, you walk across the top of the sail just as he begins to climb up. There is nowhere to go. But there is a rope hanging from the crow's nest, at the very top of the mast. Will you try and grab the rope? If so, go to **55**. Or will you try to jump down the side of the sail? If so, go to **89**.

40

With the rest of the crew drunk or asleep, you have a chance to do something as only Triton stands in your way. If you decide that the best course of action is to try to escape, turn to **45**. If you think that you have a chance to defeat Triton on your own, right now, turn to **53**.

41

You snatch Triton's time chip from the controls and without a second thought you throw it into the jungle. There is no chance, without a chip locator, that he can ever find it. You drop your chip locator on the floor and stamp on it. Then you grab a branch and smash the control panel of his time machine.

Triton hears the sound and growls deeply. Now he is trapped in 1720. His power is gone and you have beaten him. Turn to **100**.

42

There is nowhere to run and the Maroon is much bigger than you are. He tells you to take off your belt and give it to him. He looks inside the pouch and takes out the chip locator. He stares at it for a second and then throws it overboard. He then tears the pouch off the belt and stuffs it into a pocket.

You have no way of being able to find Triton now and in any case the Maroons have no use for you. The huge Maroon picks you up and throws you overboard, but before you even hit the water you feel yourself falling, falling, falling.

You find yourself on the floor of the time chamber and see Colonel Strong's face peering through the glass. Your mission is over. Strong promised that you would not come to any harm and he has kept his promise. The colonel opens the door and helps you to your feet.

'There's still time for you to catch Triton,' he tells you.

If you would like to try the mission once again, go back to **1**.

43

'I must be off; enjoy your fishing' you say and begin walking down the jetty towards the path leading to the town.

As you reach the end of the jetty you stop and watch the one-legged man throw his fishing rod into his sailing boat and then jump into the boat himself. He tugs at the rope holding the boat to the jetty and it begins to drift. A rope onboard the boat is pulled and you see the sail lift and fill with the wind and in a moment or two the boat is heading out to sea. Perhaps the one-legged man was not all that he seemed?

As the boat disappears into the distance you turn to head towards the town. Now go to **27**.

44

'Captain,' you say, 'we're not heading for Santa Diana are we?'

'No lad, the crew won't have it. They are too scared of Green and his evil pirates' the captain tells you.

'You must turn around. I will make you turn around,' you say.

'Mutiny is it!' says Captain George. 'If you beat me fair and square in a sword fight the crew will do as you say.'

He takes a sword from one of the crew and throws it to you then takes another for himself. He prepares to do battle with you.

You stare at one another for a moment and then he launches his first attack, which you beat off. You try to slice at him with the sword, but he blocks it. He makes more attacks, but each time you manage to stop him. He is too strong for you. Will you continue to fight on? If so, go to **33**. If you think that it would be better to climb up the rigging of the ship, which could give you a better chance against him, go to **39**.

45

'I'll help you however I can,' you say to the captain.

'Good lad, get some sleep – that's what I'm going to do. We've got some busy days and nights in front of us.'

You leave the captain's cabin and wait a few moments before you hear him snoring. It seems that most of the crew is also asleep, so you carefully creep into the galley and take food and drink, which you put into a sack. You then walk up onto the deck and begin lowering a lifeboat over the side.

Suddenly you hear a noise. Not all of the crew is asleep: a man has been placed on guard and he is pacing around the deck. You do not have much time. Will you hide in the lifeboat under a sheet? If so, go to **23**. Or will you continue to lower the lifeboat into the water, hoping you can do it before the man arrives? If so, go to **98**.

46

'We need to get out of here! We've got a chance to outsail him because we're faster,' you yell and Rupert nods in agreement, turning the wheel around and making the *Dragonfly* do a quick circle, heading off in the opposite direction.

The pirate ship continues to follow the *Dragonfly* but as the minutes pass it is falling behind. Do you have a compass with you? If you have, turn to **9**. If you do not, turn to **59**.

47

'Quickly, put a rowing boat over the side. I'll get him,' you shout and Mary Grey orders her men to do as you say. You jump into the boat and begin rowing. Green has a head start on you – he has already reached the beach and is running across the sand.

You try to watch him as you are rowing, looking behind you. But as he gets to the edge of the jungle you lose sight of him. You jump out of your boat as it reaches the beach and run across the sand, following his tracks. You run into the jungle and find a trail. But the trail runs left and right. Which way did he go? If you want to go left, go to **99**. If you want to go right, go to **30**.

48

You decide to give up and not risk crossing the bridge. The zombies grab you but do not hurt you. They are still moaning and making strange noises as you walk slowly towards their camp. You wonder what awaits you there. Now go to **19**.

49

The ladder to the watchtower doesn't look very safe, but you manage to climb up and onto the small platform. From here you can see the whole of the island. In the distance you can see the town of Santa Diana and beyond that the jetty. The boat carrying the townsfolk is just visible out to sea.

You look through your telescope and to your amazement you can even see a nearby island. There is a large, black shape in front of the island and you can just make out that it is a huge ship with a pirate flag fluttering in the wind. As you look again at the boat carrying the townsfolk, you see it being passed by another large ship. Its crew wear brightly coloured clothes and they are heading for the jetty.

You must warn the town, so you run back down the path and through the jungle. You reach the town, only to find that it is full of black pirates. They are escaped slaves, called Maroons.

They are not robbing the town, but they are buying food and asking about a Captain Green. They need some townsfolk to help them crew their ship. At last you have found someone who may be able to help you and you volunteer to join them. You spot a small bag of gold on the ground and snatch it up. This might be useful to bribe them to take you onboard. Now go to **63**.

50

Green's ship looms closer and closer; all the time they are firing their cannons at the *Dragonfly*. Most of the crew have already jumped overboard and soon only you and Rupert stand on deck. Together you swing the *Dragonfly's* only cannon around and manage to load it, despite the whizzing cannon balls passing over your head. You manage to fire one shot, which hits the pirate ship. By now the pirates are so close you can hear them laughing. The pirate ship swings around so that all of its cannons are facing you. You hear a clap, like thunder, and then you find yourself falling, falling, falling.

You find yourself on the floor of the time chamber and see Colonel Strong's face peering through the glass. Your mission is over. Strong promised that you would not come to any harm and he has kept his promise. The colonel opens the door and helps you to your feet.

'There's still time for you to catch Triton,' he says.

If you would like to try the mission once again, go back to **1**.

51

'That would be really exciting! What's Captain Green like?' you ask.

'He might look a little strange, but he is the finest captain I have ever served with. There'll be plenty of excitement and gold to go around,' Hop-Along Jones tells you.

In a few minutes Jones has packed his fishing rod on his boat and you are ready to set sail.

'Pull that rope youngster and I'll set the sail. We need to get to the captain's ship before dark,' he yells.

Jones lifts the sail and the wind immediately catches it. The little boat begins to move away from the jetty. In a few minutes you are in open sea and an hour later the island is just a speck in the distance.

'Where are we headed?' you ask.

'Ah, now that would be telling. We should be there soon,' Jones replies.

With little to do you settle down and watch Jones at work. He is obviously an able sailor.

An hour or so later you can see that you are headed for another island. As you get closer you can see a huge pirate ship anchored just off the shore. Jones was obviously telling you the truth. You turn your back on him and switch on the chip locator. It is picking up a very weak signal. Triton must be close. Now turn to **67**.

52

You decide that you are better off staying with Rupert and the townsfolk. You jump aboard and Rupert orders his men to set sail. After an hour or so you can no longer see the Maroons' ship and the *Dragonfly* is alone at sea.

Suddenly you see a speck in the distance. As the minutes pass the shape gets larger and larger. To your horror you see that it is a pirate ship!

'It's Green's *Emerald Dragon*. We've found them,' shouts Rupert, as he begins waving to the ship.

You hear a terrible whistling sound and within a split second you are soaked with water.

'They're firing at us! They're firing their cannons at us! Show them a white flag. That will tell them we are surrendering,' you hear Rupert order.

The pirates ignore the white flag and continue firing, their cannon balls getting closer and closer. The *Dragonfly* has just one cannon. Will you try to convince Rupert to fight? If so, go to **50**. Or will you tell him that the best thing to do is to try to escape? If so, go to **46**.

53

Although you are frightened, you walk up to Triton and tap him on the shoulder. He spins around to face you.

'I can't let you do any of that, Captain. I know exactly who you are – Triton.'

'So, Colonel Strong is sending children to defeat me now?' Triton laughs. 'Do you really think that I will let you stop me?'

Triton grabs you and carries you up to the deck. He orders two of the men to lower a lifeboat then tells you to climb over the side and jump into the boat.

'You know I can't harm you. You'll just disappear if I try,' Triton shouts down, 'but I'll cast you adrift and you'll not stand in my way.'

One of the pirates has climbed down with you and no sooner are you in the lifeboat than he kicks it away from the *Emerald Dragon* and you begin to drift off into the darkness.

You have no sail or oars, so you must allow

the sea to take you wherever it wishes. You
sleep well, despite the danger, and in the
morning you can see a tiny island off in the
distance and your lifeboat seems to be heading
in that direction. Now turn to **78**.

54

You decide to ignore the parrot, but he keeps
squawking. You continue searching the cabin.
The room is stuffed with gold, jewellery and
other things that he has stolen from ships his
pirates have attacked. You wonder what he
wants with all of these riches, but try as you
may you cannot find his time chip.

Suddenly you hear the captain's voice. He
must not realise that you
are searching his
cabin. Will you hide
in his wardrobe? If so, go to **6**.
Or will you run and hope that he doesn't spot
you? If so, go to **14**.

55

You throw your sword down into the water and grab the rope. You push yourself off from the mast and swing across. Although you don't mean to, your feet hit Captain George in the chest, knocking him off balance. He tries to hold on, but he falls and splashes into the water beside the ship.

The crew cheers and shouts, 'We've got a new captain!'

One of the crew is helping Captain George back onboard and he shakes your hand, saying, 'Where to, Captain? You won a fair fight.' Now go to **35**.

56

'Can I make you a drink, Captain?' you ask. 'Jones says you love gunpowder rum, but I'm not sure how to make it.'

'That would be splendid. Just pour out a glass of rum and top it up with some

gunpowder from the barrel.
Once you've done that, strike
a match and stand well back.'

It does seem a very strange
drink, but you follow his
instructions and place the
glass, with the gunpowder
and rum in it, on the
centre of his table. You
find a wooden stick and set
fire to the end of it from one of the
hanging lanterns. The captain has sat down
and is watching you.

'Just dip the flame into the drink, but mind
you stand back or you'll lose your eyebrows,'
he warns you.

You hold the match at arm's length and
touch the surface of the drink. It immediately
bursts into flame and there is a cloud of smoke
filling the room. The drink is still alight as
you pass it to Green and he greedily gulps
it down.

'Splendid,' he says and then promptly falls asleep.

Now is your chance to search his cabin. You switch on your chip locator and it is buzzing and flashing even more urgently than before. Now go to **58**.

57

'No!' you reply. 'I'd never become a rotten pirate!'

Jones clenches his teeth and waves his stick at you. You back away, but there is nowhere to go.

'I've told you too much. I can't let you go running to the town and warn them about the captain,' he snarls.

Jones corners you on the jetty and as he swings his stick at you, the world begins to spin. Strange shapes pass before your eyes and you feel yourself falling, falling, falling.

You find yourself on the floor of the time chamber and see Colonel Strong's face peering through the glass. Your mission is over. Strong promised that you would not come to any harm and he has kept his promise. The colonel opens the door and helps you to your feet.

'There's still plenty of time for you to catch Triton,' he tells you.

If you would like to try the mission once again, go back to **1**.

58

You begin searching the drawers of his desk and suddenly you hear a noise.

'Polly wants some seeds.'

You look around. There is no one to be seen.

'Polly wants some seeds.'

Sat on a perch in the corner of the cabin is a large scruffy parrot. It tips its head and stares at you. Will you feed the parrot? If so, go to **80**. If you decide to ignore the parrot, go to **54**.

59

Although Green's pirates have been left behind, Rupert is so terrified that he is steering the *Dragonfly* directly away. Suddenly you hear a terrible tearing sound and the *Dragonfly* grinds to a halt and begins to fill with water.

'We've hit a reef! We're all doomed!'

The boat is awash with water and the crew are jumping out to try to reach safety. In a moment, you are alone, but no one has taken the ship's lifeboat. You swing it over the side and cut the ropes with a knife that you find next to the wheel. You scramble aboard and let the waves sweep you away from the *Dragonfly* as it slowly sinks into the deep.

The waves sweep you away from the reefs and after a short while the lifeboat hits sand and you realise that it has been washed ashore. Now go to **82**.

60

'Will you help me?' you ask. 'Will you help me save Santa Diana?'

'Of course I will,' replies Mary Grey. 'But his pirate fleet is strong. How can we defeat him?' she asks.

You think for a moment. You really only have two options. If you wish to suggest that you should lie in wait for him until he attacks Santa Diana and then attack him, go to 7. If you think that it is better to attack him now, before he gets anywhere near Santa Diana, go to **86**.

61

You snatch Triton's time chip and take your chip locator out of your pouch. There is a hole  where the time chip fits and without even looking to see what Triton is doing you clip it in.

You hear a scream and a fading voice pleading, 'No, please, don't do it, don't do it …'

You look over to where Triton was standing, looking for the gold. His body is flickering and fading away. He manages one last deep growl and then disappears.

You have defeated him! Now you have his time chip for 1720 and he can never come back to Santa Diana. The world is safe, until the next time. But where will he strike and will you and F.E.A.R. be ready?

Suddenly you feel yourself falling, falling, falling.

You find yourself on the floor of the time chamber and see Colonel Strong's smiling face peering through the glass. Your mission is over. Strong promised that you would not come to any harm and he has kept his promise. The colonel opens the door and helps you to your feet.

'You've done it! You've beaten him!'
Everyone in the room is clapping and cheering.

Your F.E.A.R. mission has been a success.
You can now return home, pleased with your
work, until the next time of course. Who knows
where Triton will strike again?

62

None of the others has refused, so you cross
your fingers behind your back, hold your other
hand up and repeat his words.

'I swear on my life that I will serve my
captain for this life and the next.'

You must now drink some of the blood from
the cup, although you are pleased to discover
that it is only crushed strawberries.

Triton claps you on the shoulder and says,
'Welcome lad, we'll make a good team. You'll
be my cabin boy from now on and answer to
none but your captain.'

Now turn to 77.

63

You hand over the bag of coins to
the Maroon. He smiles at you and
says, 'You don't need to give
me these. There's
fortunes to be made for all
of us, but only if we can beat Captain Green.'

You decide to join the Maroons and leave the
townsfolk to continue their work. The Maroons
are frightened of Green, but know that they
must face him or he will seek them out and kill
them all. Two weeks ago Green's pirates
attacked their island base and burned a lot of
the houses.

Before you head off you have one last
chance to change your mind. Will you stay
with the Maroons for their help? If so, go
to **79**. If you think that your luck will be better
if you stay with the townsfolk, and join
them in their mission to try to bribe Green
onboard the little boat, the *Dragonfly*, then
turn to **52**.

64

'Where's the *Emerald Dragon*? Have we changed course?' bellows Captain George.

'Yes Captain,' replies the first mate.

The captain and the crewmen continue arguing for some time and the ship seems to be heading further out to sea. You look around and you can see no land in any direction. You have no idea whether you are headed towards Santa Diana or not. Perhaps the crew know a better route. Now turn to **66**.

65

The *Red Lady* crashes through the waves. But by now you have absolutely no idea where you are or where you are headed. Captain George seems fed up and angry with his crew and just stands on deck, staring out to sea. He has obviously lost his fight with the crew and they are not prepared to face Green.

Some time in the afternoon you hear a shout from the crow's nest, at the top of the mast. The lookout has seen an island and the *Red Lady* begins to head for it. Now go to **31**.

66

The *Red Lady* continues to make good progress, with a strong wind behind her. By now you realise that you are heading into deep water and cannot possibly be making for Santa Diana. The captain is still arguing with his crew, but they are not taking any notice of what he is saying. You have a choice whether to challenge the captain and try to convince him to turn around and head back towards Santa Diana. If you want to challenge the captain, go to **44**. If you want to say nothing, turn to **65**.

67

By the time the *Dashing Darling* pulls alongside

the huge pirate ship the chip locator is flashing and beeping.

'What's that noise? Are there mosquitoes around here? Blood-sucking insects, I hate them!' yells Jones.

You pretend to swot away a mosquito and decide it is probably best to turn off the chip locator. At least you know that Triton's time chip is close by. You will have to wait for your chance to search for it once you are onboard.

Several bloodthirsty-looking pirates throw a net over the side of the ship, so that you and Jones can climb up. He has great difficulty in doing this, with his wooden leg, and some of the other pirates are laughing at him. Perhaps Jones is not quite as important as he would like to make you think. Now go to **84**.

68

As the ship gets closer you can see that at the front it has a carved and painted figure of a woman in a red dress, with a crown on her head. You can hear shouts coming from the boat and it pulls alongside your lifeboat. You see faces peering down at you. A net is thrown over the side and two pirates, armed with swords and pistols, climb down it to carry you out of the lifeboat.

Once you are on deck they give you a mug of wonderful, cold water. As you are drinking it a tall woman walks up to you.

'I am Mary Grey, pirate captain of the *Roaring Girl*. Who are you, youngster?'

Leaving out the bit about Triton being an evil alien, you quickly explain your story. She smiles and says, 'I hate Captain Green. There's never been a more evil pirate. He gives us good pirates a bad name.'

Now turn to **60**.

69

'I'll not swear anything to you,' you reply.

'You won't then!' Green shouts. 'So you'll walk the plank and I'll have done with you!'

Before you can move, one of the crew has grabbed you by the shoulders and picked you up, taking you to the ship's rails. A plank has already been placed over the side, just in case anyone refused. He pushes you out onto it.

You still have one last chance to change your mind. If you wish to swear the captain's oath, go to **62**. If you still refuse, go to **28**.

70

Several townsfolk have already volunteered to join the crew. You step forward and join them. They look like very capable sailors, but you are certain that trying to bribe Triton will not work.

There are eight of you and by the time you have reached the jetty, a boat called the *Dragonfly* has come alongside and several sailors are preparing it for the voyage. Food is being put onboard and a large chest of gold is being lifted over the side.

The man who will captain the boat is the mayor's son, Rupert. He and the others are very frightened, but up for the challenge and determined to save their town. They think that the mayor's plan will work and they have high hopes that Santa Diana will be saved from the pirates.

After about half an hour the boat is ready to leave. Quickly the *Dragonfly* moves away from the jetty and heads out to sea. They have no real idea where Captain Green and his pirates are hidden. They hope that by searching the nearby islands they will find signs of him. Many of the crew are very scared, but see no other way to deal with the pirates. Now go to **32**.

71

The zombie king orders his men to go to their ships. There are at least 20 creaking ships, covered in seaweed and slime. But somehow they all manage to float. You join the zombie king on the largest of the ships and set sail to find Captain Green's pirates.

The zombie king passes you a telescope and says, 'You keep a lookout. Your eyes are better than mine.'

So you stand at the front of the ship, looking this way and that to try to spot Green's pirates. Suddenly you see a ship heading towards you. You do not recognise it.

To your horror, as the boat nears you can see the skull and crossbones flag fluttering in the wind. It is a pirate ship! But is it Green? Now turn to **85**.

72

Running as fast as you can, you see that you are catching him up. You can see his red jacket ahead of you. On the ground is his hat, which must have fallen off. As you turn a corner in the

Date due

Current time: 29/08/2019,
15:12
Title: The crime lord :
choose your own adventure
Author: Shadow, Jak.
Item ID: 3909556680
Date due: 19/9/2019,23:59

--- Items Renewed Today ---

Library name: HW Gayton
Library (Harrow)
User ID: 24102004172152

Current time: 29/08/2019,
15:12
Title: The Emerald Pirate
Author: Shadow, Jak.
Item ID: A802901217827
Date due: 19/9/2019,23:59

Total issues for session:1
Total issues:2

Thank you.

trail you see a strange machine. It looks like a car without any wheels and Triton is loading his last chest of gold into it. Even now he is climbing into the machine and is ready to leave. It must be Triton's time machine.

You have only two options. You can either try to trick him or rush at him. Will you trick him by shouting and telling him he has forgotten a chest of gold? If so, go to **21**. Or will you try to run and take him by surprise? If so, go to **83**.

73

The key doesn't seem to fit any of the locks. They are all the wrong shape. But eventually you do find a lock it fits – on a long, thin chest beside the captain's bed. You turn the key and unlock the chest. Inside is a chart with 13 arrows, all pointing to Santa

Diana. At the end of each arrow is the name of one of Triton's pirate ships. He must have 12 pirate captains and their ships under his command. This is Triton's plan to attack Santa Diana from all directions.

What is strange is that your chip locator is no longer bleeping or flashing. You realise that it was only working when Triton was near. He must have the time chip on him and has not left it in the cabin. You put the chart back into the box and re-lock it, making sure that you remember to clip the key back onto the parrot's chain. Now go to **22**.

74

You hide, shaking under the bush. Now you can see dozens of zombies, all with torches. One of them stops just beside the bush and sniffs the air.

'Man. I smell man,' you hear. The other zombies stop and sniff the air too. They begin to search for you.

All of a sudden a zombie sees you and several of them rush and grab you and begin to take you back to their camp. They do not have a strong grip, so there is a chance for you to escape. Will you try to escape now? If so, go to **93**. If you decide not to struggle, go to **19**.

75

You watch several of the townsfolk step forward and volunteer to crew the boat. Perhaps it might be the best plan for them, but not for you. You decide that you need to explore the island a little more and, perhaps, see if there are any signs that the pirates are already here, or close by.

You leave Santa Diana's town and take a path through the jungle, which seems to be heading towards the middle of the island.

The path is quite steep so you know that you are heading up a hillside. After about an hour's walk you reach the top of the hill. The trees here have been cut down and there is an abandoned watchtower. You decide that this is the best place to be able to view the whole area, so you climb it. At the top you find a bag of coins. Thinking they might be useful, you pick them up and add them to your possessions.

You then look around you. If you have a telescope, go to **49**. Otherwise you will not be able to see very much and have only one real option and that is to join the crew. You must head back to Santa Diana and go to **70**.

76

In the blazing sun you raise your telescope to
your eye and begin to look north, south, east
and west. At first you think you might have
spotted a bird, way off in the distance. But as
you continue to stare through the telescope the
shape is getting larger. It is a ship heading in
your direction. You cannot escape and you
have no idea who the boat belongs to.

To your horror, as the boat nears you can
see the skull and crossbones flag
fluttering in the wind. It is a
pirate ship! But is it Green?
Now turn to **68**.

77

To celebrate, the captain orders ten barrels of rum to be brought up for the crew. In a very short time everyone is drunk and they are dancing and singing, except for Captain Green and yourself.

'Come down to the cabin and, now I can trust you, I'll tell you everything,' says Captain Green.

You follow him to his cabin and he takes his key from the parrot's chain and opens his chart box, laying out his plan on his table.

'You'll have noticed that I am not like other men,' says the captain.

You nod, unsure quite what to say in reply.

'Let's just say I don't come from these parts. In fact, I don't come from this time,' he says. 'I belong in your future, but here is where I'll win my war. We're headed for Santa Diana. It's a poor and useless island in this time. But in the future my enemies have used it as their base.' You pretend to look shocked and amazed.

'If my men can take the island in this time, I can send them into the future and we can

seize the island and my enemies will be destroyed. I'll see you're safe, but never betray me,' he warns.

'Of course I won't, Captain,' you answer, smiling inside. Now you know all of his plans. Turn to **40**.

78

The wind is definitely blowing you towards the island. It has a deserted, sandy beach and beyond that the rest of the island seems to be covered in jungle. There is no sign of anything, and slowly, but surely, the waves take your boat closer to the beach, until it finally comes to rest on the sand. Now turn to **82**.

79

You decide to board the *Red Lady* and ask Captain George whether he will help you in defeating Captain Green.

'No one will be safe on any of the islands, not even you, if we don't stop Captain Green,' you explain.

'I know that and I'll help you as best I can. But first we have to find him. What we do then will be up to the crew.' Now turn to **95**.

80

You walk over to the parrot. There is a bowl of seeds and grapes beside his perch and one at a time you begin passing him seeds. He holds each one in his claw and nibbles at it with his beak. You can see that the parrot has a chain around his other leg, stopping him from flying away. Halfway down the chain is a tiny key.

While the parrot is busy with a grape, you bend down and unclip the key from the chain. You wonder which lock it fits. Now go to **73**.

81

The man is sound asleep and is snoring. He has only got one leg and his wooden leg looks as if a dog has chewed it. He looks harmless enough, so you give him a shove.

'What's up? Who are you?' he growls.

You don't answer. It is best not to tell anyone anything until you know who or what they are.

'Where am I? Which way is the town?' you ask.

'You're on Santa Diana of course, where else? The town is about five minutes' walk from here. Funny questions to ask me, not knowing where you are or where you're going,' the man grumbles.

You decide to tell him your name, but nothing else. After all, you don't know who he is or why he is here. He seems to own the boat that is tied up to the jetty. Do you want to continue talking to the man? If so, go to **37**. If you do not want to talk to him anymore and want to go Santa Diana's town, go to **43**.

82

You are alone on the deserted island. It is covered with heavy jungle and it is already getting dark. You walk back to the lifeboat and find a hook and line, so at least you might be able to catch yourself a fish for your supper. After half an hour you give up. None of the fish seem interested, so you walk back towards the edge of the beach, where the jungle begins. You find a coconut at the foot of a tree. You pick it up, hit it against a rock and drink the creamy milk inside.

You decide to settle down for the night and explore the island in the morning. No sooner have you shut your eyes than you hear strange drumming in the distance. As the minutes pass the drumming gets louder and louder.

Will you hide and wait for the drumming to get closer? If so, turn to **26**. If you decide to investigate the drumming, turn to **96**.

83

As you run towards his time machine he slams the door shut and begins to laugh. His hand moves towards a switch and the time machine flickers. There is a blinding light and the machine, Triton and the gold disappear into the future. At least he has not destroyed Santa Diana, but perhaps he will return. Suddenly you feel yourself falling, falling, falling.

You find yourself on the floor of the time chamber and see Colonel Strong's face peering through the glass. Your mission is over. Strong promised that you would not come to any harm and he has kept his promise. The colonel opens the door and helps you to your feet.

'I almost completed the mission' you say to Strong. 'I was so close to catching Triton.'

If you would like to try the mission once again, go back to **1**.

84

As soon as you get onboard ship you immediately recognise Triton. He is walking towards you. He is a lot bigger than you thought he would be and he has two pistols stuffed into his belt. He is wearing a bright red jacket, with blue and gold cuffs. He has a red handkerchief with white spots tied around his head and a huge captain's hat, with a blue feather sticking out of it. He does look like a pirate captain, except for the fact that his skin is green.

'Aah, just what I could do with – a cabin boy. I need someone to keep my quarters shipshape. Welcome aboard the *Emerald Dragon,* the finest ship you'll find in these parts. Are you up for adventure and gold?' he asks.

'Yes I am, Captain' you reply.

'Excellent,' he replies. 'Follow me.'

As Triton turns, Jones whispers in your ear. 'The captain loves his gunpowder rum. If you want to stay in his good books I'd make him one if I were you.'

Captain Green's quarters are full of padlocked chests, maps, compasses and charts.

Your room is next door to his quarters and it seems to be comfortable enough.

Will you ask him whether he would like some gunpowder rum? If so, go to **56**. If not, go to **13**.

85

The front of the boat has a carved, wooden figure of a woman in a red dress. Quickly, you tell the zombie king.

'It is Captain Grey and the *Roaring Girl*. They are our friends,' he explains.

In moments the *Roaring Girl* is alongside the zombie king's ship and a tall woman swings over and jumps onto the deck. She tells you she is Mary Grey and Green is her enemy. She is one of the tallest women you have ever seen and she looks very strong. At a distance you would mistake her for a man.

She is wearing plain grey trousers and a blue jacket that is buttoned to the neck, even though it is very hot. Her hat is pushed back from her face and she has a lovely, welcoming smile.

'Will you help me?' you ask. 'Will you help me save Santa Diana?'

'Of course I will,' replies Mary Grey. 'But his pirate fleet is strong. How can we defeat him?' she asks.

'We must make good speed,' shouts the zombie king. 'We want to hunt for Green now.'

You decide that you are better off with Mary Grey. At least you won't sail straight into a trap, so you leave the zombie ship and hope that the zombie king will keep his promise.

You think for a moment. You really only have two options. If you wish to suggest that you should lie in wait for Green until he attacks Santa Diana and then attack him, go to 7. If you think that it is better to attack him now,

before he gets anywhere near Santa Diana,
go to **86**.

86

'I think we should attack him straight away,'
you say.

'We'll attack him at his base. He won't know
we're coming, so we'll have a chance,' says
Mary Grey.

The *Roaring Girl* heads towards Green's base
on a nearby island. There are 13 of Green's
pirate ships anchored near the beach. The
Roaring Girl comes in close and several of the
pirates on the other ships wave a welcome.

Suddenly the *Roaring Girl's* cannons fire,

ripping huge holes into the sides of the pirate ships. In a few minutes five of them are sinking and there are pirates jumping from the ships and trying to swim to the beach. The *Roaring Girl* turns around and fires the cannons from its other side, sinking three more.

Green's ship, the *Emerald Dragon,* has managed to slip away and is heading for the open sea. You tug at Mary Grey's arm and point.

'He's getting away!'

'What shall we do?' she asks.

Do you think the *Roaring Girl* should chase him? If so, go to **4**. Or do you think you still need to protect Santa Diana as he may escape you and head for the island? If so, go to **10**.

87

'I think that we'll have a better chance if Green doesn't know that we are already here,' you say. Mary Grey nods and the mayor agrees with you.

Mary Grey orders the crew of the *Roaring Girl* to take her around the side of the island where they are to anchor in a bay and wait for a signal.

Have you met the zombie king? If you have, go to **3**. If you have not then you should go to **29**.

88

You do not know how much use the zombie king will be. But when he shows you that he has his own ghost fleet of ships, crewed by zombies, and tells you that they all hate Green, you realise that you may have a chance. The zombie king wants to attack Green now, rather than sail to Santa Diana and protect the island.

You have a choice. You can either sail to attack Green's fleet with the zombies. If so, go to **71**. Or you can ask the zombie king to give you food and drink and make your own way to Santa Diana. If so, go to **34**.

89

Throwing your sword into the water, you use both hands to grab hold of the sail and begin to slide down. The sail is wet and slippery and you begin to lose your grip. You feel yourself falling, falling, falling.

You find yourself on the floor of the time chamber and see Colonel Strong's face peering through the glass. Your mission is over. Strong promised that you would not come to any harm and he has kept his promise. The colonel opens the door and helps you to your feet.

'You were doing so well,' he says. 'You were getting close to the time chip and there's still time for you to catch Triton.'

If you would like to try the mission once again, go back to **1**.

90

'Fire at him! He mustn't escape!' you shout.

Mary Grey orders her men to fire the cannons.

The shots whistle towards Green but splash harmlessly around his lifeboat. You have no option. You must chase him and take the time chip from him. Turn to **47**.

91

A compass could be useful as the needle will always tell you which way is north and you

can work out which ways are south, east and west. It is a good choice because you may well find yourself at sea, or perhaps in the jungle on an island.

As long as you know where you should be heading, the compass will always be useful to tell you which way you need to go.

'I think I'll take the compass,' you say.

'It's a good choice and it's easy to keep it safe,' replies Colonel Strong, smiling.

You put the compass into your pouch, along with the chip locator. Now go to **16**.

92

The wind and waves rock the boat this way and that. The rain lashes at your face. As suddenly as it began the storm stops and the sun begins to beat down on you once again. You have absolutely no idea where you are. The storm could have blown you way off course.

You feel weak and tired and very thirsty. Slowly you begin to drop off to sleep and then you feel yourself falling, falling, falling.

You find yourself on the floor of the time chamber and see Colonel Strong's face peering through the glass. Your mission is over. Strong promised that you would not come to any harm and he has kept his promise. The colonel opens the door and helps you to your feet.

'You were doing so well,' he says. 'You were getting close to the time chip and there's still time for you to catch Triton.'

If you would like to try the mission once again, go back to **1**.

93

Without warning, you pull yourself free and run from the slow-moving zombies. You crash through the jungle, but you can still hear the zombies moaning and groaning behind you. You can see their torchlight flickering to your left and right. You can only run forwards.

Eventually the jungle stops and in front of you is a swaying, wooden bridge over a deep canyon. You can hear the water rushing over rocks below you. Will you risk crossing the bridge? If so, go to **15**. Or will you surrender to the zombies and take your chances? If so, turn to **48**.

94

It seems that you might not have any choice as to whether or not you head for Santa Diana. The sea's waves seem to be taking you towards what looks like a deserted island.

The wind is definitely blowing you towards the island. It has an empty, sandy beach and beyond that the rest of the island seems to be covered in jungle. There is no sign of anything and slowly, but surely, the waves take your boat closer to the beach. Finally it comes to rest on the sand. Now turn to **82**.

95

Captain George and the crew are very friendly and not quite what you expected pirates to be like. They are simply happy to be free and on the seas with no other master, except themselves. They hate Green because two weeks ago his pirates attacked their island and burned many of their homes. You have no idea what direction the *Red Lady* is heading in. But the captain has promised that he will search for Green.

After a couple of hours sailing you realise he has been telling the truth. Ahead, in the distance, is a large pirate ship. It is coming towards you.

'That's the *Emerald Dragon*, so we've found Green all right. What shall we do?' asks Captain George.

The crew don't look too happy, but Captain George says to you, 'Let's have a private word about all this in my cabin. I don't want the crew to overhear us.'

You decide that it is best for Captain George and his crew to pretend to join Captain Green's pirate army. At least that way you would know what he is doing and will have a chance to grab the time chip.

You have only been below deck for a few minutes, but when you and the captain walk back on deck, the *Emerald Dragon* has disappeared. If you have a compass, turn to **25**. If you do not have a compass, turn to **64**.

96

Although it is dark, you decide to investigate the drumming noise. As you walk along the path through the jungle, the drumming is getting louder and just ahead you can see flickering torchlight. You stop for a second and now you can hear a dreadful moaning noise. The jungle is too thick for you to leave the path and the torchlight is getting closer. The drumming is louder and the awful moaning noise is all around you.

Suddenly, just ahead of you on the path, you see a terrifying sight. It is a man holding a torch and moaning. His eyes are blank. You have met the living dead! The zombie sees you and several others rush and grab you and begin to lead you away. They do not have a strong grip, so there is a chance for you to escape. Will you try to escape now? If so, go to **93**. If you decide not to struggle, go to **19**.

97

The *Roaring Girl* heads off from Santa Diana. Holding a telescope to your eye, you look in every direction to see if you can find Green's fleet. In the far distance you see smoke and as the *Roaring Girl* gets closer you hear cannons being fired. It is a sea battle. The zombie king has attacked Green's pirates. The *Roaring Girl* joins the fight, firing her cannons into the first of Green's ships. The pirate ship topples over and begins to sink. The crew cheer and you look to see if you can find Green's own ship, the *Emerald Dragon*.

It has slipped away from the battle and is trying to make for Santa Diana. Will you chase it? If so, go to **4**. Or will you ignore the *Emerald Dragon* and decide to head back to the island? If so, go to **10**.

98

You continue to lower the lifeboat down the side of the *Emerald Dragon*. The guard is now very close and can hear you.

'Alarm! Alarm!' he shouts and you hear several pirates running towards you.

'What's going on here? This boy must be a spy! Throw him over the side!' shouts one of the pirates.

Two of the pirates grab you and begin swinging you in their arms. As they throw you over the side you can feel yourself falling, falling, falling.

You find yourself on the floor of the time chamber and see Colonel Strong's face peering through the glass. Your mission is over. Strong promised that you would not come to any

harm and he has kept his promise. The colonel opens the door and helps you to your feet.

'You were doing so well,' he says. 'You were getting close to the time chip and there's still time for you to catch Triton.'

If you would like to try the mission once again, go back to **1**.

99

You choose to head along the trail that leads to the left. You run along the track, hearing parrots squawk and flutter all around you. The track opens out into a large, cleared area where you find an old church, which is burned and deserted. There are no signs of Green.

You've gone the wrong way. You need to run back along the trail and take the right turning. Now turn to **30**.

100

There is a strange glow around Triton and his body begins to disappear. You hear him screaming 'No!'. He has been transported back to his own future. Suddenly you feel yourself falling, falling, falling.

You find yourself on the floor of the time chamber and see Colonel Strong's smiling face peering through the glass. Your mission is over. Strong promised that you would not come to any harm and he has kept his promise.

The colonel opens the door and helps you to your feet.

'You've done it! You've beaten him!' he says. Everyone in the room is clapping and cheering.

'Colonel, we've found agent 107. He has turned up on the coast of Cuba and he has just managed to get to a telephone. A helicopter should be picking him up now,' says one of the agents.

'It seems our work is done in 1720, well done, I'm glad everyone is safe,' replies a relieved Colonel Strong.

Your F.E.A.R. mission has been a success. You can now return home, pleased with your work, until the next time of course. Who knows where Triton will strike again?

The Spy Master

Triton has become Gary Steel – a criminal mastermind! He has kidnapped the inventor Albert Fudge and is forcing him to build the ultimate computer to take over the world.

Can YOU discover Steel's secret base and destroy the computer? YOU solve the puzzles and find the clues in this exciting adventure into the world of spies.

£4.99   ISBN 1 84046 692 8

The Space Plague

It is 600 years in the future and the inhabitants of Earth have started travelling to other galaxies.

Triton and his vile henchmen have infected the planet Rosetta, home to many humans, with a deadly plague.

YOU are sent forward in time to visit Rosetta with the only known cure. Can YOU battle with aliens to reach the distant planet on time? YOU are the settlers' only hope, but danger lurks everywhere! Solve the puzzles and find the clues in this exciting adventure into future alien worlds.

Published October 2005

£4.99   ISBN 1 84046 694 4

The Crime Lord

Triton has become the Crime Lord of London! His army of child thieves are robbing the capital. Even the best police detectives are powerless – they need help.

YOU are sent back into the foggy streets of Victorian London to solve the baffling case and bring Triton's grip on the city to an end. Can YOU discover Triton's secret lair? Can YOU stop him? Solve the puzzles and find the clues in this exciting adventure.

Published October 2005

£4.99   ISBN 1 84046 693 6

Fighting Fantasy™

Fighting Fantasy™ is a brilliant series of adventure gamebooks in which YOU are the hero.

Part novel, with its exciting story, and part game, with its elaborate combat system, each book holds many adventures in store for you. Every page presents different challenges, and the choices you make will send you on different paths and into different battles.

Magic and monsters are as real as life in these sword-and-sorcery treasure hunts which will keep you spellbound for hours.

There are over 20 *Fighting Fantasy*™ titles available.

Click on www.fightingfantasygamebooks.com to find out more.

Suitable for readers aged 9 and upwards

Fighting Fantasy™
The Warlock of Firetop Mountain

Deep in the caverns beneath Firetop Mountain lies an
untold wealth of treasure, guarded by a powerful
Warlock – or so the rumour goes. Several adventurers
like yourself have set off for Firetop Mountain in search
of the Warlock's hoard. None has ever returned. Do
you dare follow them?

Your quest is to find the Warlock's treasure, hidden
deep within a dungeon populated with a multitude of
terrifying monsters. You will need courage,
determination and a fair amount of luck if you are to
survive all the traps and battles, and reach your goal –
the innermost chambers of the Warlock's domain.

£4.99   ISBN 1 84046 387 2

Suitable for readers aged 9 and upwards

Fighting Fantasy™
Eye of the Dragon

In a tavern in Fang, a mysterious stranger offers YOU the chance to find the Golden Dragon, perhaps the most valuable treasure in all of Allansia. But it is hidden in a labyrinth beneath Darkwood Forest and is guarded by the most violent creatures and deadly traps.

To begin your quest YOU must drink a life-threatening potion, and to succeed you must find maps, clues, artefacts, magic items, jewels and an imprisoned dwarf.

£4.99   ISBN 1 84046 642 1

Suitable for readers aged 9 and upwards

Football Fantasy

Football Fantasy is a stunning new series of football gamebooks in which YOU decide the outcome of the match. YOU see what a footballer would see and make the decisions he would make.

Simple to play and challenging to master, every game is different. Learn the tricks and tactics of the game and lead your team to victory.

All titles £5.99

Thames United	ISBN 1 84046 598 0
Mersey City	ISBN 1 84046 597 2
Medway United	ISBN 1 84046 599 9
Trent Albion	ISBN 1 84046 590 5
Bridgewater	ISBN 1 84046 609 X
Clyde Rovers	ISBN 1 84046 621 9
Avon United	ISBN 1 84046 622 7
Tyne Athletic	ISBN 1 84046 596 4

Suitable for readers aged 10 and upwards